NORMAN WHITNEY
The Truth Machine

HEINEMANN

HEINEMANN GUIDED READERS
BEGINNER LEVEL
Series Editor: John Milne

The Heinemann Guided Readers provide a choice of enjoyable reading material for learners of English. The Series is published at five levels – Starter, Beginner, Elementary, Intermediate and Upper. At **Beginner Level**, the control of content and language has the following main features:

Information Control
The stories are written in a fluent and pleasing style with straightforward plots and a restricted number of main characters. The cultural background is made explicit through both words and illustrations. Information which is vital to the story is clearly presented and repeated where necessary.

Structure Control
Special care is taken with sentence length. Most sentences contain only one clause, though compound sentences are used occasionally with the clauses joined by the conjunctions 'and', 'but', and 'or'. The use of these compound sentences gives the text balance and rhythm. The use of Past Simple and Past Continuous Tenses is permitted since these are the basic tenses used in narration and students must become familiar with these as they continue to extend and develop their reading ability.

Vocabulary Control
At **Beginner Level** there is a controlled vocabulary of approximately 600 basic words, so that students with a basic knowledge of English will be able to read with understanding and enjoyment. Help is also given in the form of vivid illustrations which are closely related to the text.

For further information on the full selection of Readers at all five levels in the series, please refer to the Heinemann Guided Readers catalogue.

1
Success for Professor Verity

'Success!' cried Professor Verity. 'My new invention is ready. It is now complete. I shall call it The Truth Machine.'

The professor ran to the telephone and phoned the newspaper office. He told them about the Truth Machine.

'Come to my laboratory,' he said. 'You will see my new invention. I call it the Truth Machine.'

'Please give us your name and address,' said the girl at the newspaper office. 'We'll send a reporter immediately.'

The professor gave the girl his name and address.

'Will the reporter be here soon?' he asked.

'Yes, of course,' replied the girl.

'Good,' said Professor Verity. He smiled. He waited.

The reporter soon arrived at the laboratory.

'Who can use the Truth Machine, Professor?' he asked.

'Anybody can use it,' replied Professor Verity.

'But how does the machine work?' asked the reporter.

The professor laughed. 'That's a secret,' he said. 'But I can tell you this. The questioner sits in the little chair. I sit at the controls. And the truth speaker sits in the big chair. The truth speaker always speaks the truth. He cannot tell lies.'

The professor smiled.

'Why did you make the Truth Machine?' asked the reporter.

'I love truth,' said Professor Verity, 'and I hate lies. I love good people and I hate bad people. I love peace and I hate war. The Truth Machine loves truth, good people and peace. It hates lies, bad people and war.'

The reporter wrote all this in his notebook.

'Soon everybody will know about the Truth Machine,' said the professor. 'It will be a success.'

The reporter thanked the professor and hurried back to his newspaper office.

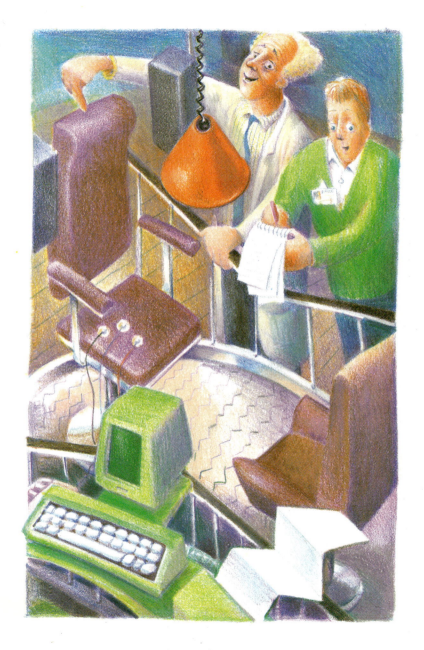

Professor Verity was right. Soon, millions of people knew about the Truth Machine.

The professor was on the radio. He was on the television too. All over the world, newspapers and magazines wrote about Professor Verity and the Truth Machine.

Many people wrote to Professor Verity. Rich people, poor people, young people, old people — everybody sent letters. The Truth Machine was a success!

'Thank you,' wrote one woman.

'Wonderful,' wrote another.

'Good Luck!' wrote one man. 'I am sending you some money. It will help your work.'

Many people sent money. Some sent coins. Others sent banknotes. And others sent cheques and money orders.

Then the professor chose his first clients. He read his letters many times. First, he chose a hundred letters. Then he chose fifty of them. Then he chose ten names. Finally, he chose three people: Mrs Seeker, from Australia; Inspector Sack, from South America; and Dr Simple, from the United States.

Professor Verity wrote to them.

'Please come and see me,' he wrote. 'You will be one of my first clients.'

2
Three Visitors for Professor Verity

Two weeks later, Professor Verity had a visitor. It was Mrs Seeker. She was from Australia. She was a housewife. She was afraid.

'Can I help you, Mrs Seeker?' asked the professor.

'Yes,' Mrs Seeker replied. 'I wrote to you about the Truth Machine.'

'I know,' said the professor. 'You will be my first client. Don't be afraid.'

'Oh!' said Mrs Seeker. 'I will not be your first client, Professor. Your first client will be my husband!'

'Your husband!' said Professor Verity. The professor was surprised. 'But your husband didn't write to me.'

'No, he didn't,' said Mrs Seeker. 'I wrote to you.'

'But what do you want?' asked the professor. 'Why are you here?'

'Well,' said Mrs Seeker. 'My husband . . .'

Mrs Seeker stopped. She was crying. She was unhappy.

'My husband has . . .' Mrs Seeker stopped again. She was crying again.

'Oh!' said the professor quietly. 'Your husband has . . . another woman!'

'Yes, yes,' cried Mrs Seeker. 'But I don't know. Oh, I hate lies. I want the truth, Professor. I want the truth from my husband.'

'But will he come here?' asked the professor.

'Oh yes, he'll come,' said Mrs Seeker.

'Well, bring him to my laboratory,' said the professor. 'I'll help you, Mrs Seeker. Of course, there will be a small charge, a fee.'

'I'll pay anything,' said Mrs Seeker. 'I hate lies. I want the truth from my husband.'

'Come here next Monday morning,' said the professor. 'Everything will be ready.'

The next visitor was Inspector Sack. He was from South America. He was a policeman and he had a gun.

'Hello, Professor,' said the inspector.

The inspector had a loud voice.

'Where is it, Professor?' he shouted. 'Where is the Truth Machine?'

'It's here, Inspector,' said Professor Verity quietly. 'You will be one of my first clients.'

'Ah, good,' said the inspector.

Inspector Sack walked up and down. Then he stopped. He looked at the professor.

'Crime!' shouted Inspector Sack. 'Crime! Crime! Crime!'

'Crime?' asked the professor in a soft voice.

'Yes! Crime!' shouted Inspector Sack. 'I hate criminals. Murderers are criminals. They kill people. I hate murderers. Thieves are criminals. They take things from people. I hate thieves. And liars are criminals. They tell lies. I hate lies, Professor. I hate all criminals.'

'But the Truth Machine will fight criminals,' said Professor Verity quietly. 'There will be no more murderers and thieves. There will be no more lies and no more crime, Inspector!'

'No more criminals, and no more crime!' shouted Inspector Sack. 'Excellent!'

'Bring your criminals to me, Inspector,' said the professor. 'Of course, there will be a small charge, a fee.'

'Money?' shouted Inspector Sack. 'You shall have money, Professor. We are fighting crime, my friend. Of course you shall have money.'

'Thank you, Inspector,' said Professor Verity. 'Thank you. Come here next Monday afternoon. Bring your criminals to me. Everything will be ready.'

'Good morning, Professor Verity. My name is Dr Simple.'

Dr Simple was the third visitor. He was from the United States. He was a government official. He worked for the American government.

'Hello, Dr Simple,' said the professor. 'You will be one of my first clients.'

'I know,' said Dr Simple. 'I will be your third client. The other two are Mrs Seeker and Inspector Sack.'

'Oh?' said the professor. 'How do you know their names?'

Dr Simple looked round.

'Spies, Professor Verity,' said Dr Simple quietly. 'Spies!'

'Spies?' asked Professor Verity. 'But Mrs Seeker and Inspector Sack aren't spies.'

'Of course they are not spies,' said Dr Simple. He looked round. 'But I am.'

'Oh, you are a spy?' the professor asked.

'Yes,' said Dr Simple. 'I'm a spy.'

He looked round. He was looking for enemy spies.

'I fight for peace,' said Dr Simple.

Professor Verity smiled.

'Oh, I want peace too,' the professor said.

'I know,' said Dr Simple. He smiled. 'You will help me, Professor. We have caught an enemy spy. He will not tell the truth. I will bring him here. I will be the questioner. He will be the truth speaker.'

'Yes,' said the professor. 'Please bring him here. Of course, Dr Simple, there will be a small charge, a fee.'

Dr Simple smiled. He looked round again. 'Of course, Professor. Here is some money.'

Dr Simple gave the professor a lot of money.

'Thank you,' said the professor quietly. He looked round too. 'Come here with your spy next Monday evening. Everything will be ready.'

3

Monday. A Busy Day for Professor Verity

It was Monday morning. Mrs Seeker came to the laboratory. Mr Seeker came too.

'Hello, Professor,' said Mr Seeker. 'Where is your Truth Machine?' Mr Seeker laughed.

'Don't laugh,' said his wife. She was afraid. 'Listen to the professor.'

Professor Verity spoke. 'Mrs Seeker, you are the questioner. Sit in the small chair. Mr Seeker, you are the truth speaker. Sit in the big chair.'

Mr and Mrs Seeker sat in their chairs. Mrs Seeker looked at the professor.

'What shall I say?' she asked.

'Ask your husband some easy questions,' said the professor.

She looked at her husband. 'What is your name?' she asked.

'My name is Henry,' said her husband. 'That was an easy question!' he laughed.

'How old are you, Henry?' asked Mrs Seeker.

'I'm . . . er . . . I'm forty-seven,' said Mr Seeker.

Mrs Seeker looked at Professor Verity. She smiled.

'That's the truth!' she said. 'He usually says forty-three. My husband is telling the truth.'

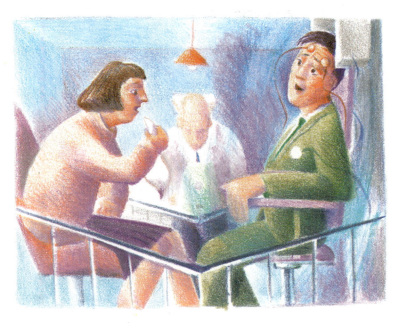

'Good,' said Professor Verity. 'Now ask your husband some difficult questions.'

Mrs Seeker was afraid. But she spoke.

'Are you married?' she asked.

'Of course I'm married,' replied Mr Seeker. 'You're my wife.' He was angry.

'But – but – do you love me?' asked Mrs Seeker.

Mr Seeker looked at his wife. She waited.

'No . . .' he said slowly. 'No . . . I don't love you. I love another woman.'

'Oh!' said Mrs Seeker. 'Who do you love? Tell me the truth. I hate lies. Who do you love?' Mrs Seeker was crying.

Mr Seeker looked at his wife. 'I love Anne Elliott. I love Anne Elliott!' he said.

Inspector Sack came to the laboratory on Monday afternoon. His boss, the Chief Inspector, came too. They brought some criminals with them.

'Good afternoon, Professor!' shouted Inspector Sack. 'This is my boss, the Chief Inspector. And these are the criminals. They are murderers. They are thieves. And they are liars.'

'But today,' said Professor Verity, 'they will tell the truth.'

'Shall we begin?' said the Chief Inspector, quietly.

'Yes, let's begin. Come on!' shouted Inspector Sack.

Inspector Sack sat in the questioner's chair. The first

criminal sat in the truth speaker's chair. Inspector Sack spoke. 'Did you take money from the car of Señor Cavalho?' he asked.

'Yes, I took the money,' said the criminal.

'Guilty!' shouted Inspector Sack. 'Five years in prison. Next criminal.'

The next criminal sat in the truth speaker's chair.

'Did you take diamonds from the house of Señorita Reggia?' asked Inspector Sack.

'Yes, I did,' said the criminal.

'Guilty!' shouted the inspector. 'Ten years in prison. Next criminal.'

The next criminal came in. He sat in the truth speaker's chair.

'Did you kill Señor Rey?' asked Inspector Sack.

The criminal was silent. Then he spoke. 'Yes, I did,' he said. That was the truth.

'Guilty!' shouted Inspector Sack. 'Twenty years. Next!'

All the criminals sat in the truth speaker's chair. They all told the truth. One of them was innocent.

'You are not guilty,' said Inspector Sack. 'You can go home.'

Inspector Sack was pleased. Professor Verity was pleased. The Chief Inspector was pleased.

'Good work, Sack,' said the Chief Inspector. 'Very good work.'

'Thank you, sir,' said Inspector Sack. 'We are fighting crime, sir! The Truth Machine is helping us. There are no more criminals for us, sir!'

Inspector Sack smiled. He was happy.

It was Monday evening. Dr Simple came to the laboratory. Another man came with him. The other man was a spy.

'Good evening, Professor,' said Dr Simple.

'Good evening, Dr Simple,' said the professor. 'Everything is ready.'

'Good,' said Dr Simple. 'This spy is dangerous. He is an enemy. I will be his questioner. He will be the truth speaker. He will tell the truth.'

The professor went to the controls. Dr Simple sat in the questioner's chair. The spy sat in the truth speaker's chair.

'What is your name?' asked Dr Simple.
'My name is Harville Lyme,' said the spy.
'Where are you from?' asked Dr Simple.
'I am from Russia,' said the spy. The spy smiled. Dr Simple looked at the professor. Dr Simple was pleased.
'Excellent, Professor Verity,' said Dr Simple. 'Lyme is telling the truth. He will tell me everything.'
Professor Verity was happy.

Dr Simple looked at Lyme. 'Are you a spy?' he asked.

'Yes, I am a spy. I am an important spy,' said Lyme.

'Do you know the secret of the new military aircraft?' he asked.

Harville Lyme smiled. 'Yes,' he said. 'I know the secret of the new military aircraft. And my government knows too.'

'Ah!' cried Dr Simple. 'The Truth Machine is wonderful. This spy is telling me everything.'

'But I have another secret,' said Lyme. He looked at Dr Simple. He looked at Professor Verity.

'Another secret?' cried Dr Simple. 'Tell me. Tell me. Tell me the truth!'

'My secret is this,' said Harville Lyme. 'I never tell the truth. I always tell lies.' He smiled.

4
Tuesday. An Important Meeting

There was a hotel near the laboratory. Mrs Seeker was staying there. Inspector Sack and Dr Simple were staying there too. Mrs Seeker, Inspector Sack and Dr Simple were eating breakfast together.

'I know the truth about my husband. Now I am very unhappy,' said Mrs Seeker.

'I know the truth about my criminals. Now I haven't got a job,' said Inspector Sack.

'I know the truth about my spy. What shall I do now?' said Dr Simple.

Mrs Seeker was crying. 'I don't like the Truth Machine,' she said. Inspector Sack and Dr Simple agreed with her.

Inspector Sack shouted in a loud voice. 'We paid the professor a lot of money,' he said. Mrs Seeker and Dr Simple agreed with him.

Dr Simple spoke quietly and slowly. 'Professor Verity is a criminal,' he said. Mrs Seeker and Inspector Sack agreed with him.

'I'm going to see Professor Verity,' said Mrs Seeker.

'I shall come with you,' shouted Inspector Sack.

'A good idea,' said Dr Simple slowly. 'I shall come too.'

Mrs Seeker, Inspector Sack and Dr Simple left the hotel. They wanted to see Professor Verity. They went to the laboratory.

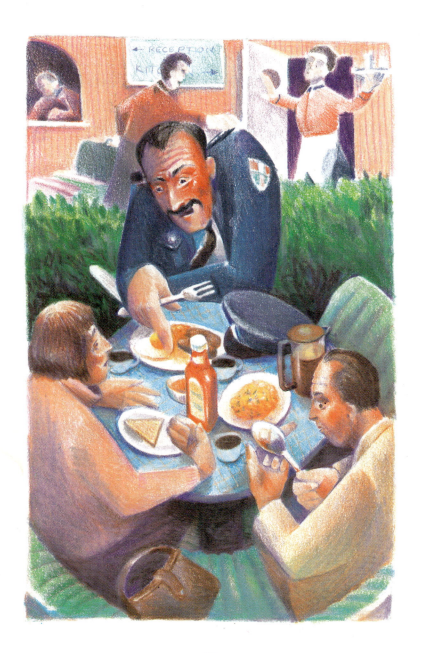

5

At The Laboratory Again

Soon Mrs Seeker, Inspector Sack and Dr Simple were at the laboratory.

'Oh, I hate you, Professor Verity!' cried Mrs Seeker.

'I want my money back, Professor!' shouted Inspector Sack.

'You are a criminal, Verity!' said Dr Simple.

Professor Verity looked at his first three clients. 'Fools!' he said. 'You are fools. You wanted the truth. I gave you the truth. The Truth Machine gave you the truth.'

'Truth?' said Mrs Seeker. 'But now I am unhappy!'

'Truth?' shouted Inspector Sack. 'But now I haven't got a job!'

'Truth?' said Dr Simple. 'But what is the truth?'

'What is the truth?' said Professor Verity. 'Let me tell you!'

'Mrs Seeker! You hate lies and I gave you the truth. Your husband loves Anne Elliott. That is the truth!

'Inspector!' the professor went on. 'You hate crime. I put your criminals in prison. That is the truth.

'Simple!' said the professor. 'You fight for peace. I helped you. That is the truth.'

The professor stopped. Then he spoke again. 'Fools!' he said. 'Go home.'

'Do you really hate lies, Professor Verity?' asked Mrs Seeker.

'Do you really hate crime, Professor?' shouted Inspector Sack.

'And do you really fight for peace?' asked Dr Simple.

'Yes! Yes! Yes!' cried Professor Verity. 'That's the truth.'

Then Dr Simple spoke. 'We shall see,' he said. 'Professor Verity will be the truth speaker!'

'You don't hate lies, Professor Verity. You want success,' said Mrs Seeker.

'You don't hate crime, Professor. You want money,' shouted Inspector Sack.

'You don't want peace, Verity, you want power,' said Dr Simple.

'Yes!' laughed Professor Verity. 'You fools! You gave me success. You gave me money. You gave me power. Now I am successful, rich and powerful. And that is the truth!'

Everybody was quiet. Then Inspector Sack took out his gun. Mrs Seeker screamed. Inspector Sack shot Professor Verity. And Dr Simple destroyed the Truth Machine.

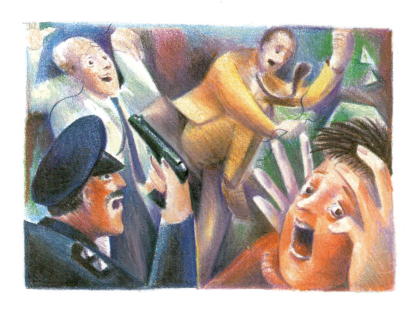

Heinemann English Language Teaching
A division of Heinemann Publishers (Oxford) Ltd
Halley Court, Jordan Hill, Oxford OX2 8EJ

OXFORD MADRID ATHENS PARIS FLORENCE PRAGUE
SÃO PAULO CHICAGO MELBOURNE AUCKLAND
SINGAPORE TOKYO GABORONE
JOHANNESBURG PORTSMOUTH (NH) IBADAN

ISBN 0 435 27176 8

© Norman Whitney 1976, 1992
First published 1976
Reprinted eight times
This edition published 1992

A recorded version of this story is available on cassette.
ISBN 0 435 27283 7

All rights reserved; no part of this publication may be
reproduced, stored in a retrieval system, or transmitted, in any
form or by any means, electronic, mechanical, photocopying,
recording or otherwise, without the prior written permission of
the Publishers.

Illustrated by Peter Tucker
Typography by Adrian Hodgkins
Cover by Peter Gudynas and Threefold Design
Typeset in 12/16 pt Goudy
by Joshua Associates Ltd, Oxford
Printed and bound in Malta